BACKPACKER.

Trailside
Navigation

BACKPACKER

Trailside
Navigation

MAP AND COMPASS

Molly Absolon

Photographs by Dave Anderson

FALCONGUIDES

GUILFORD, CONNECTICUT
HELENA, MONTANA

AN IMPRINT OF GLOBE PEQUOT PRESS

FALCONGUIDES®

Copyright © 2010 by Morris Book Publishing, LLC

Backpacker is a registered trademark of Cruz Bay Publishing, Inc.

FalconGuides is an imprint of Globe Pequot Press.

Falcon, FalconGuides, and Outfit Your Mind are registered trademarks of Morris
Book Publishing, LLC.

Text design by Sheryl P. Kober
Page layout by Melissa Evarts

Library of Congress Cataloging-in-Publication Data

Absolon, Molly.
  Backpacker magazine's trailside navigation : map and compass / Molly Absolon.
    p. cm.
  Includes index.
  ISBN 978-0-7627-5654-4 (alk. paper)
  1. Orienteering. I. Backpacker. II. Title. III. Title: Trailside navigation.
  GV200.4.A27 2010
  796.58—dc22

                                                            2009046677

Printed in China

10 9 8 7 6 5 4 3 2 1

Contents

Chapter One:
Introduction to Trailside Navigation   1

Chapter Two:
Topographic Maps   8

Chapter Three:
Compasses and Altimeters   34

Chapter Four:
Dividing the World   44

Chapter Five:
Global Positioning Systems (GPS)   50

Chapter Six:
Route Finding   56

Index   79

Topographic maps help you plan your route, anticipate hazards, calculate travel times, and envision your destination.

Chapter One
Introduction to Trailside Navigation

Before I go into the mountains, I like to pull out all the maps for the area where I'm heading, lay them across the floor, and dream. The intricate twisting brown contour lines, white snow patches and bright blue lakes, the trails or lack of trails winding through the landscape—all are enough to get my adrenalin going. I try to identify potential routes that will take me away from the main thoroughfares, over obscure passes and into places that seem off the beaten track. I spend hours perusing the possibilities, conjuring up images of what I might see if I were there: Cliffs, rivers, glaciers, forests—that information and more is laid out in front of you on a topographic map.

If you've driven a car, you have undoubtedly used highway maps. These maps also show roads, trails, rivers, lakes, and other relevant features, but they give no indication of the topography you may encounter. Roadmaps just show you a flat world, which for driving is fine; you don't really need to know whether you are going uphill or down when your automobile is doing all the work. But once you lace up your boots, throw on a backpack, and start walking, every up and down makes a difference. You want—really, need—to know what the landscape looks like before you set off to cross it on foot. For this kind of navigation, you need a topographic map.

Topographic maps create a two-dimensional picture of a three-dimensional world. With a little practice, topographical maps give you a sense of the place you are going and the things you will encounter en route. You can use a map to predict travel times, to anticipate challenges or obstacles, to pick out camping spots or rendezvous points, to choose a fishing hole or a cliff to climb, or just to excite your imagination about the infinite possibilities for adventure represented on the page.

Take time to look around and orient yourself to the landscape. You'll start to recognize macro features and general trends in the topography that help you develop your internal sense of direction.

BEYOND YOUR MAP

Backcountry navigation requires more than just the ability to use navigational tools. You also need to develop your sense of direction. People who have lived or traveled in a given area for an extended period of time learn to recognize key signs that help clue them in to where they are: The mountains trend north-south, for instance, or most streams flow in an easterly direction to empty into one major river. Such clues can help you recognize the cardinal directions—north, south, east, and west—before you pull out your map and compass.

The sun can also be helpful in orienting yourself to your surroundings. If it is late afternoon and you are walking into its glare, you know right away you are heading west. Some backcountry travelers use the stars to help guide them, but I like to think I'll be comfortably in camp before I have to resort to locating the North Star to get my bearings. Mind you, it's fun to know where the North Star is, but I don't know very many backpackers who actually use it as a navigational tool. Still, these macro signs are helpful in developing your navigational skills. If you've been paying attention to the lay of the land

Look at your map frequently to develop an accurate sense of scale and to keep track of your whereabouts.

as you hike, you are unlikely to be completely disoriented when it comes time to bring out the map to figure out where you are and where you are going.

For most backpackers topographic maps are all you really need to navigate the wilderness, but there are other tools—a compass, an altimeter, a GPS—that can fine-tune your navigational skills and allow you to pinpoint your position with a degree of precision that may be critical at certain times, such as when following a bearing to paddle to an unseen island or when telling a pilot exactly where you are located.

But don't get too hung up on using a compass or Global Positioning System (GPS) when a map and your intuition will suffice. I remember traveling through the canyons of southeastern Utah with a man who insisted on following a bearing because that is what he'd been trained to do. It made absolutely no sense to me, as we were obviously boxed in by canyon walls and as long as we continued downstream, there was no way we could get lost. Our best navigation trick was to count side canyons as we passed them. I think by the end of the day my colleague too was convinced that in some places a compass is not that helpful.

Like so many things in life, trailside navigation is an art, not a science. You need to master the tools and learn the language, but ultimately, good backcountry travelers develop an eye that allows them to see the landscape from the lines on the map. This book is the first step in helping you develop your own navigational eye.

SPECIFIC NAVIGATION TOOLS

In this book we will introduce the basic, critical tools you need for navigating in the wilderness. These tools include, first and foremost, a topographic map.

Most backcountry travelers also carry a compass. Compasses contain a magnetic needle that automatically points to magnetic north, allowing you

Compasses are useful for orienting your map.

to orient yourself in the event you become confused about your whereabouts. You can use a compass to align your map to the landscape. Or you can shoot a bearing—either a visual bearing off the land or a bearing from your map—that will lead you to your destination. Both skills will be explained in this book.

We will also discuss the use of altimeters for navigation. Altimeters indicate elevation, which can be helpful when you know you are somewhere on a slope or pass but can't pinpoint your location from the landforms around you. Having an elevation point can allow you to home in on your precise position.

Finally, we will introduce readers to a GPS receiver, which uses satellites to identify your location and allows you to outline a path on your map or overland. GPSs are a great way to locate precise points, such as a rendezvous spot or a trailhead, where accuracy is critical.

Using the Tools

You can have an intellectual understanding of these tools but still be lost in the mountains if you don't know how to use them in the field. Orienting a map from the landscape or following a compass bearing takes practice and skill. This book includes basic steps and exercises to allow you to teach yourself these skills and give you the confidence to venture out into the wilderness on your own reconnaissance.

So let's get started.

Chapter Two
Topographic Maps

WHAT IS A TOPOGRAPHIC MAP?

All maps depict a portion of the earth's surface graphically. What makes topographic maps different from a regular road map is that they show topography, or the shape of the land. Landforms—mountains, valleys, ridges, and hills—are depicted through the use of contour lines, or lines that connect equal points of elevation. To visualize what a contour line represents, take a rock and submerge part of it into a cup of water. The line that marks the break between wet and dry is a contour interval, or a point of equal elevation on that rock.

The gold standard for American topographic maps is the United States Geological Survey's (USGS) maps. The USGS took over the mapping of the United States in 1879 and has been its primary mapping agency ever since.

The best-known USGS maps are the 1:24,000-scale topographic maps, also known as 7.5-minute quadrangles; 7.5-minute maps have been made for all 48 contiguous states and Hawaii. In Alaska 7.5-minute maps are only available for areas around Anchorage, Fairbanks, and Prudhoe Bay. The rest of the state is covered by 15-minute maps and contain less detail because of their smaller scale.

The 7.5-minute mapping program was completed in 1992 and has subsequently been replaced by the National Map program, a collaborative effort between the USGS and a variety of governmental and private partners to deliver geographic information through the Internet as downloadable data. However, paper copies of 7.5-minute quads remain available and are one of the most useful types of maps for backcountry travelers because of their great detail and accuracy.

This book will focus on understanding USGS 7.5-minute maps. At the end of this section, we'll introduce other types of topographic maps you may encounter in your travels, but the map-reading principles you use are the same, regardless of the brand or scale of your map.

Information on the Margins

The information in the margins of your map is critical background data. Here's where you'll find the map's name, location, scale, date of issue, and other relevant information. Most hiking trips are going to take you across more than one 7.5-minute quadrangle, so you'll need to know what other maps are in the area in order to make sure your entire trip is covered. Scale and contour intervals are invaluable to understanding how far you can travel and what kind of terrain you should expect to encounter en route. In some areas where the land is flat and featureless, contour intervals can be as low as 10 feet, while in other mountainous regions you may find maps with 80-foot or greater contour intervals. That can make a big difference if your intended path takes you over forty contour lines in the course of a day. On a map with 80-foot contours, that means you'll be climbing 3,200 feet, while on one with 10-foot contours, you'll only go up 400.

Date

The date on a map is also a vital piece of information. For example, Aspen, Colorado, has changed dramatically since 1960 when the map in the illustration on the following pages was first made. Most of these changes are man-made rather than natural; you don't really expect a mountain to alter its shape in fifty years, but trails get rerouted, new buildings appear, and bridges may come and go, so it's

What's on the Map Margins?

Start by looking at the margins of your map to locate several key pieces of information; specifically the map's name and scale; its latitude, longitude, and UTM location; the names of adjoining maps; and the date. On this map the **name** is Aspen, Colo. (a) and the **date** is 1960 (b), with photo revisions made in 1987. The **scale** of the map is 1:24,000 (c), which means one inch on the map represents 24,000 inches on the ground. Below this number there is a **graphic scale** (d). For 7.5-minute maps, one inch on the map equals 2,000 feet, which translates to 2.6 inches on the map

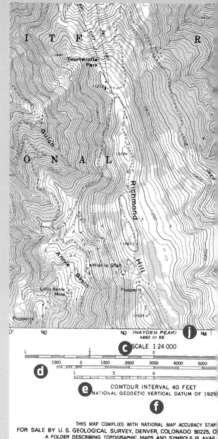

equating to one mile on the ground. The **contour interval** (e), or the distance in elevation between contour lines, is 40 feet. Below the contour interval you'll find the datum used for the map (f). This map uses the National Geodectic Vertical Datum. **Latitude and longitude** (g) can be found in the map corners. For example, in the lower right-hand corner of this map, you'll find the latitude is 106°

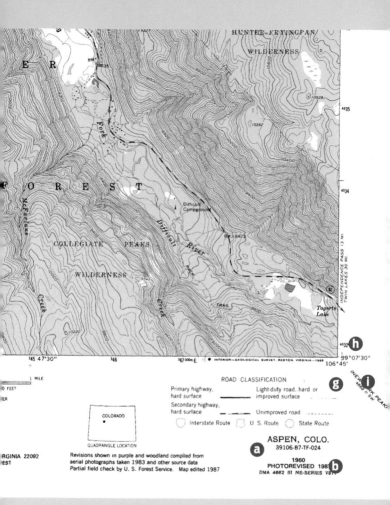

HUNTER–FRYINGPAN
WILDERNESS

FOREST

Difficult Campground

BM X8473

COLLEGIATE   PEAKS

WILDERNESS

TRAIL

Taggert Lake

INDEPENDENCE PASS 13 MI.
TWIN LAKES 30 MI.

h

45 47'30"   346   347 000m E   ● INTERIOR–GEOLOGICAL SURVEY, RESTON, VIRGINIA–1988

99°07'30"
106°45'

g

i

(NEW YORK PEAK
4662 III SW–SERIES V877)

1 MILE

0 FEET

ER

COLORADO

QUADRANGLE LOCATION

RGINIA 22092
EST

Revisions shown in purple and woodland compiled from
aerial photographs taken 1983 and other source data
Partial field check by U. S. Forest Service. Map edited 1987

ROAD CLASSIFICATION

Primary highway,
hard surface

Secondary highway,
hard surface

Light-duty road, hard or
improved surface

Unimproved road

◯ Interstate Route   ◯ U. S. Route   ◯ State Route

ASPEN, COLO.
39106-B7-TF-024
a

1960
PHOTOREVISED 198 **b**
DMA 4662 III NE–SERIES V877

45' west, while latitude is 39º 7' 30" north. Intermediate lat/long
marks are found both up the side and along the bottom of the map.
(h) The UTM zone and grid for this map is also found in the map
corners. The **adjacent map,** "New York Peak" (i), lies immediately
to the southeast of this map, while the "Hayden Peak" (j) quad is
due south.

important to know how old the map is before you rely too heavily on ephemeral data to pinpoint your location or choose a route.

The Aspen map was photo revised in 1987, which means some changes will be shown in purple, but 1987 was still more than twenty years ago, so you are likely to encounter other modifications on the ground that do not appear even in the revised version. The bottom line is this: If the map is more than ten years old, be wary of man-made features or any other variations that could have taken place in the intervening years.

Declination Diagram

On all maps the top points north. Compasses, however, actually point to magnetic north, which varies from a few degrees up to 30 degrees off from true north. The specific angle of this variation is determined by your location; therefore, it will be different for different

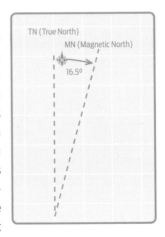

maps. You'll find a graphic representation of this difference in the margin at the bottom of your map. This is called the declination diagram. The line topped by a star points to true north, the one topped by MN points to magnetic north, and a third line capped by GN, points to Grid North. We will discuss these features in more detail in the compass navigation section.

Color

Cartographers have been using color to provide information on maps for hundreds of years. You may encounter some variations in the specific hues found on different maps, but in general basic color designations haven't changed much since the 1400s.

» **Black:** Indicates man-made features such as buildings, roads, surveyed benchmarks, and labels for towns, peaks, rivers, etc.

» **Red:** Used for more prominent man-made features such as surveys, boundaries, and major highways.

» **Brown:** Used for contour lines to identify relief features and for elevation markers.

» **Blue:** Identifies hydrological features such as lakes, rivers, swamps, and ponds. A dashed blue line enclosing a white area indicates permanent snowfields or glaciers.

» **Green:** Indicates vegetation with military significance (most topographic maps were originally created for military purposes). This means vegetation that can hide or encumber troop movements, such as forests, orchards, or scrub.

» **Other:** Occasionally, other colors may be used to show special information, such as purple for photo revisions. These colors are usually explained in the marginal information.

Common Symbols

Topographic maps are remarkably intuitive once you've played around with them a bit. A curved line with small hatch marks radiating off the top looks like a grass hummock and is. These symbols are used for indicating swampy areas. Buildings are black squares, while a black square with a cross represents a church. Still, it is helpful to familiarize yourself with some of the more common symbols shown here so you can interpret your map with more accuracy and precision.

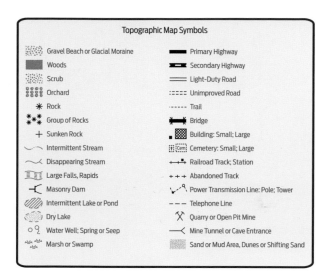

Topographic Map Symbols

Symbol	Description	Symbol	Description
	Gravel Beach or Glacial Moraine		Primary Highway
	Woods		Secondary Highway
	Scrub		Light-Duty Road
	Orchard	:::::	Unimproved Road
✳	Rock	------	Trail
✳✳✳	Group of Rocks		Bridge
+	Sunken Rock		Building: Small; Large
	Intermittent Stream	Cem	Cemetery: Small; Large
	Disappearing Stream		Railroad Track; Station
	Large Falls, Rapids	+ + +	Abandoned Track
	Masonry Dam		Power Transmission Line: Pole; Tower
	Intermittent Lake or Pond	– – –	Telephone Line
	Dry Lake	✕	Quarry or Open Pit Mine
o ♀	Water Well; Spring or Seep		Mine Tunnel or Cave Entrance
	Marsh or Swamp		Sand or Mud Area, Dunes or Shifting Sand

USING YOUR MAP: CONTOUR LINES

As we've explained before, contour lines connect equal points of elevation. That's a simple enough definition, but learning to actually interpret these lines—that is, to translate the wiggles on your map into a mountain or valley—takes some skill.

Get out a map and look at the contour lines. Without much effort, you can pick out steep terrain where the lines get crammed together and flat terrain where big blank spaces appear. Every fifth contour line will be darker than the intermediate lines and is known as an **index contour.** The elevation of the index contours appears printed along each line at regular intervals. On many 7.5-minute USGS maps,

Knuckle Mountain

One of the best ways I've seen to explain contours is to use your hand as a mountain. Make a fist. Take a marker or pen and carefully trace a line that stays level around each individual knuckle. Make these lines at regular intervals; say, a quarter of an inch apart. Don't let the line dip down between fingers, or climb up over finger bones. You'll find you must angle up into the "valley" between your fingers

the contour interval is 40 feet, with index contours occurring every 200 feet.

Occasionally, on maps representing flat terrain, the cartographer may include supplementary contour lines, which are represented as dashed brown lines. These lines indicate one-half the contour interval, or 20 feet if the contour interval is 40.

to stay level (forming a "V" that points uphill) and then must move out over the "ridges" represented by each finger (forming a "V" that points downhill). Once you've drawn a series of lines at various elevations, flatten your hand. Now you will see the topographic map of your hand: a two-dimensional representation of your three-dimensional fist.

Recognizing Landforms

Probably the best way to learn to recognize landforms is to take a map, go outside where you have an expansive view, and pick out landmarks. This exercise helps you develop a sense of the map's scale and an eye for how physical features appear when transcribed into contour lines.

First, pick out a nearby mountain or hill and describe its shape. Does it have a steeper side? Are there cliffs visible? Do you see valleys where streams run off? Is it a flat-topped mountain or does the peak have a distinctive pyramid shape at the summit? Do forests blanket its sides?

Now find the mountain on your map and look at how these characteristics are depicted. You'll notice ridges have distinctive V shapes that point downhill. Summits appear as closed circles, and cliffs may have disappearing lines where the rock is overhanging.

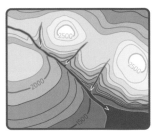

Here you can see a fairly steep-sided river valley. If you had looked at this landscape before consulting your map, you'd probably have decided that the best walking route was on the southern side of the river, on the open slope. The map reinforces this viewpoint, showing little room along the riverbanks for hiking, while the southern slope is gradual and should allow easy travel.

This illustration shows how the contour lines depict features in the land. Steep slopes have lines close together, circles represent mountaintops, passes between peaks are depicted by the pinching of lines, and valleys are represented by kinks or "V's" in the contour lines that point uphill.

Take care to observe and describe your surroundings *before* consulting the map to avoid the potential pitfall of making the land fit the map.

Now look at a valley. Does the valley have a river or stream in the bottom? Can you see where the stream meanders through flat meadows? Or is it pinched in and flowing straight down through a steep-sided canyon? Do any side streams flow in? Are there trees or swampy areas?

After you have described the valley, look at it on the map. You'll notice that the contour lines for big, wide-bottomed glacial valleys fold back in a gentle U shape that points uphill, while in steep-sided canyons the contour lines wrap back around themselves tightly into narrow Vs.

To ensure you know exactly where you are, take the time to describe at least five land features surrounding your location before you consult your map.

If you can subsequently identify each of those features on your map, you can be fairly confident you've pinpointed your location correctly.

**Five Identifying Characteristics
for Determining Location**

» Proximity to water
» Slope angle
» Tree cover
» Aspect
» Major landforms (peaks, drainages, meadows, etc.)

PLANNING A ROUTE

Most backcountry travelers usually—wisely—stick to trails or established routes on their initial forays out into the wilderness. But even if you plan to be on a trail all day, it behooves you to look carefully at the map before you set off. It's all too easy to blast through a trail junction and end up miles off track if you aren't paying attention and haven't identified some key landmarks to keep track of your progress.

The first step is to pinpoint your starting location. Now, using a stick or some kind of pointer, trace your planned route carefully, making note of key features you will pass on the way. These features can help keep you on track just as a handrail on a staircase helps guide you. A backcountry handrail may be a river that

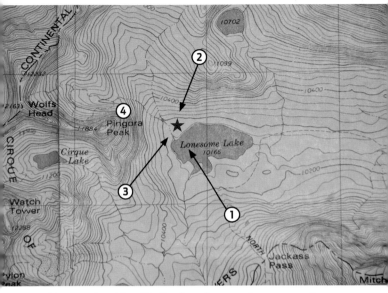

This campsite—identified by the red star on the map—can be pinpointed by four key characteristics: (1) its location at the northwestern end of Lonesome Lake; (2) in a relatively flat, open meadow; (3) near the main inlet to the lake. (4) The campsite is east of Pingora Peak.

you will be following for several miles, or you may be contouring around a peak so the slope angling off to one side will be your handrail. If you find yourself with a river on your right side when it should be on your left, or if you are traveling upstream when you were intending to go down, you know something is wrong.

A landing, on the other hand, is a point you can tick off as you go by just as landings on a staircase indicate the passage of floors. Say you notice that you

will cross a trail junction a few miles after you begin hiking. You know you have hit your landing when you come to that point. A river crossing or the top of a pass are other landings that are helpful in keeping track of your progress.

Make note of these handrails and landings before you set out. Anticipate when you should reach a specific spot (tricks on how to determine travel times are in the next section of this chapter), and observe the terrain as you hike, checking off handrails and landings as you pass them. Keep track of your time as you travel, and notice when you come upon specific features. If you thought you would reach a river crossing an hour or two after leaving camp, and you find yourself four hours out without any sign of water, you probably need to reevaluate your position to make sure you have not gone astray.

I recommend hiking with a map in your hand or in an easily accessible pocket. This allows you to consult the map readily, especially if you find the land isn't fitting into the picture you had created before you set out. Such discrepancies may reflect a failure of your imagination, or they may be warning signs that you have lost track of the appropriate trail.

Measuring Distance

You can eyeball distances roughly on a map, but for a real sense of how far you have to go and how long it will take to travel that distance, you need to be a bit more methodical in your measurements. An easy trick is to take a piece of parachute cord or string and lay it against the graphic scale diagram at the bottom of your map. Mark off miles along the cord with a permanent marker. Now you have a flexible measuring stick that makes calculating distances easy.

Calculating Travel Time

Place one end of your string measuring stick at your starting location and hold it in place. Use the cord to trace your path, taking care to follow the bends and twists in the trail. Once you've reached your destination, count up the miles your route entails.

On average, most hikers average 3 miles per hour on a trail. Your pace slows down considerably if you have a lot of elevation gain during the day, however. So before you jump to the conclusion that a six-hour trip down the trail is going to take you two hours, make sure you look at the elevation gain the route entails.

The best way to calculate elevation gain is to follow your route counting the contour lines you will cross. You don't really need to count elevation loss, as traveling downhill usually does not slow you down. And losing elevation does not negate elevation gain, so just because you climb 1,000 feet and then lose 1,000 feet does not mean your net gain is zero. You still need to factor in how that 1,000-foot elevation gain is going to affect your travel time to come up with an accurate sense of when you can expect to reach camp.

So count up the contour lines along your route and come up with a total number. For example, over the course of the day, you will gain a total of 2,200 feet. In general, a gain of 1,000 feet equates to approximately 1 extra mile of travel. So in this scenario you should estimate an additional 2.2 miles of travel time. If your linear mileage was 6 miles, plus an extra 2.2 miles for elevation gain, you will travel the equivalent of 8.2 miles, which should take two and a half hours total to travel. You'll want to build in some cushion time for rest breaks, lunch, or scenic side trips, so in reality you'll probably want to allow yourself three and a half to four hours to travel the distance.

Anticipating Hazards

Even if you plan to stay on trails, wilderness travel involves some potential hazards. In the mountains you can anticipate trails crossing boulder fields or fording rivers. High elevation passes are notorious for lightning in the afternoon, and marshy areas in early spring may mean slow going through mud and bogs.

Look closely at your route and make note of potential hazards you may encounter. For example, say you are on a trip in the Wind River Mountains of Wyoming in early June. The sales clerk at the outdoor store in a nearby town says snowline is just above 10,000 feet, but the days are warming, and things are melting fast. Your prospective line of travel for the day involves an 11,000-foot pass, with a steep

In early season when mountain snows are melting rapidly, rivers that drain large areas like this one can be difficult or impossible to cross.

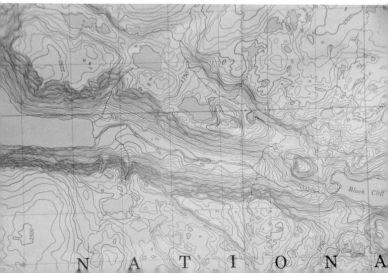

Snow-covered boulders are notorious for hiding so-called "elephant traps," or places where the snow is rotten and will not support the weight of a hiker, resulting in potentially dangerous falls.

descent on a north-facing slope. You then plan to drop down along a river that drains five major valleys. The trail fords the river above a small canyon.

Your map is not going to give you a precise picture of what conditions you will find as you travel, but you can make some fairly accurate guesses based on elevation, aspect, and weather. First, you know you can expect to run into snow on the pass, since snowline is at 10,000 feet. Many passes in the Wind Rivers are bouldery, and late-season snow in boulders can be tricky. Therefore, you should anticipate postholing and slow going in places. The steep descent on a north-facing slope is almost certainly going to be snow covered in early June, and you may need an ice ax to descend safely.

The river is likely to be swollen with snowmelt if the days have been warm and it drains a large area.

You may find it difficult or impossible to ford the stream, and the canyon downstream is an added danger if you happen to fall during the crossing.

Depending on your experience level and equipment, you may decide your route is not feasible at this time of year and you need to find an alternative destination.

COMMON MAP-READING MISTAKES

The most common mistake all map readers make at some point in their career is the trap of wishful thinking. We've all been there: You're beat, your feet hurt, your pack is getting heavier by the minute, and with a little creative imagination, you can convince yourself that you really have hiked 5 miles and are now standing smack in the middle of your predetermined destination. You know the lakeshore doesn't seem exactly right, and you thought the hill on the south side of the lake was going to be steeper, but it has to be right. After all, you were only traveling 5 miles today and it's been six hours since you left camp. It doesn't matter that you all decided to nap at lunch for two hours or that scouting the river crossing took longer than you thought it would take. You still should have covered 5 miles by now.

If you recognize these thought patterns, you are not alone. It's easy to convince yourself you are where you want to be and not that difficult to reinterpret the

Tricks for Avoiding Common Map-Reading Errors

» Check your map frequently.
» Note the time you pass specific handrails or landings. Recalculate your arrival time if you are moving slower or faster than anticipated.
» Observe the landscape before you pull out your map. Describe things verbally.
» Have five identifying landforms in mind before you begin trying to find your location on the map.
» Don't dismiss an obvious conflict.

landscape around you to fit the place you want to be on the map. We've all overestimated how quickly we are traveling and convinced ourselves that we've covered the distance, when in reality we still have a mile or 2 to go.

Finally, many novice—or out-of-practice—map readers have an inaccurate sense of scale and really can't tell how large a hill or meadow should be from its representation on the map. Look at big, obvious features first and then focus down on the more detailed features. Don't dismiss contradictory evidence. It's highly unlikely mountains have moved or the sun is setting in the east just because you want to be at your camp. You are just not reading the map correctly.

OTHER TYPES OF MAPS

In addition to smaller-scale USGS maps (such as 15-minute maps), you can now buy commercial topographic maps—hiking maps—for many popular destinations across the country. These maps are often made on waterproof paper and cover a larger area than a 7.5-minute map, thereby allowing you to carry fewer maps to cover your trip. However, they are often smaller scale, such as 1:48,000, which means 1 inch on the map equals 48,000 inches on the ground or twice as many inches as a 7.5-minute map. Many of these maps have shaded landforms that help the peaks and valleys pop out. This shading is not critical, but it can help you visualize dimensions and depth quite effectively.

Also, you can now buy software mapping programs for your computer that allow you to customize your maps. Some outdoor retail stores have these programs, allowing you to purchase customized maps without having to replace your own with the software or a large printer.

CARE OF YOUR MAP

Unless you have a map printed on waterproof paper, you should carry your maps in a plastic bag to protect them.

Folding Your Map

Lay your map on a flat surface, fold it lengthwise in half with the printed side facing in. Now fold these halves back on themselves so the printed side now faces out. The map should now be folded into fourths lengthwise. Find the map name. Now bend the folded map in half again so the name is hidden on the inside. Fold the two ends back on themselves, ending up with a small square with the map name facing out.

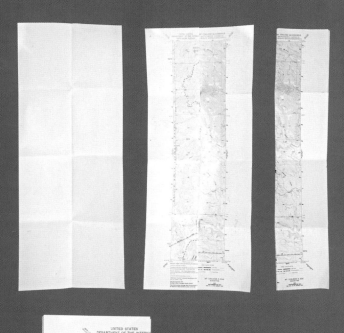

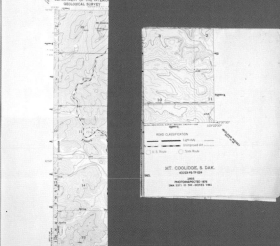

Chapter Three

Compasses and Altimeters

A compass is simply a device that indicates direction. A floating needle within the compass points to magnetic north, allowing you to orient yourself and your map to the surrounding landscape. This information is particularly useful when visibility is obscured either by weather or trees.

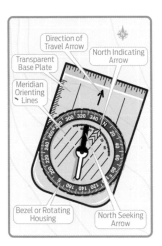

A basic, functional compass needs to have a bezel or rotating housing with an external ring printed with a compass rose indicating degrees and the cardinal directions: north, south, east, and west. Within the bezel you need a north-seeking arrow that floats in a fluid-filled capsule and a north-indicating arrow printed on the bottom. The base plate of the compass should be clear and have a direction-of-travel arrow printed on its surface.

BOXING THE NEEDLE

The first step in using your compass is to orient it so that it is pointing to magnetic north and the bezel is aligned correctly. To do this, you box the needle, or

Boxing the needle

"put the guard in the guardhouse" (the guard being the red north-seeking arrow). Hold the compass in the palm of your hand, and rotate the bezel until north lines up with the direction of travel arrow on the base plate. Now, keeping the compass level, turn your body until the red north-seeking arrow is "boxed" in by the north-indicating arrow printed on the bottom of the compass housing. Your compass is now oriented to your present location.

DECLINATION

The difference between true north at the top of your map and north as indicated by your compass needle is known as declination and reflects the angle between magnetic north and true north at your specific location. Declination diagrams are found along the bottom margin of your map.

To align your compass with true north, shift the bezel to the right or left of north the number of degrees indicated in the declination diagram. If you are in the Rocky Mountains, this means magnetic north is east of true north. The angle varies, but for the sake of an example, let's say magnetic north is east of true north by 10°. To adjust your compass, turn the dial to the left or west of north by 10° or to 350°. You then box the needle. Your direction of travel arrow will now be pointing toward true north.

Another way to use a compass is to box your needle, then align the edge of the compass with the arrow pointing toward magnetic north in the map's declination diagram.

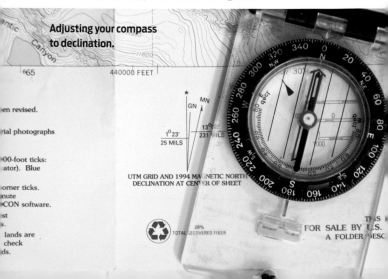

Adjusting your compass to declination.

ORIENTING YOUR MAP

To orient your map with a compass, follow these basic steps:

1. Set the compass dial to account for declination, as described above.

2. Align the edge of the compass base plate with the printed edge of your map.

3. Rotate the map and compass until the needle is boxed.

4. Your map is now oriented precisely to true north.

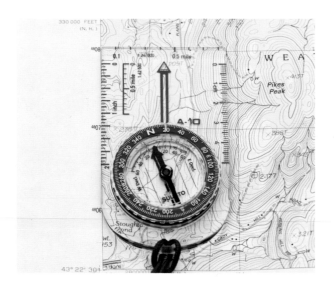

TAKING A BEARING FROM YOUR MAP

Sometimes it can be difficult to navigate without using your compass. For example, hiking through dense forests or across flat mesa tops where the land is relatively featureless and visibility may be obscured. Crossing open water in a boat or traveling in fog can be challenging without some way to keep track of your direction of travel; it will also test your ability to follow your course using landmarks alone. In these situations it can be very helpful to know how to shoot and follow a bearing.

The first step in shooting a bearing is to orient your map to true north. Then draw a line between your location and your desired destination. Now place the edge of your compass base plate along the line and turn the bezel until you have boxed the needle. The number on the bezel dial that lines up with your direction of travel arrow is your bearing.

To follow this bearing, keep the dial set with your bearing lined up with the direction of travel arrow. Now, holding your compass at waist level, rotate your body until the needle is boxed. Your direction of travel arrow is now pointing you toward your destination. Most likely, however, your path will be blocked by obstacles, making it impossible for you to just walk forward in a straight line all the way to your intended destination. So to allow for easier travel, pick out a landmark—one as distant as possible—along your projected line of

travel, walk to that landmark and repeat. You can use trees, rocks, even people sent ahead to stand along the path if nothing else will serve.

You can take a bearing from the land simply by pointing your compass at a landmark, and boxing the needle. Again, the number that lines up with the direction of travel arrow will be your bearing. But if you can see your landmark, you probably don't need to take a bearing to reach it. Shooting a bearing off the land is usually most

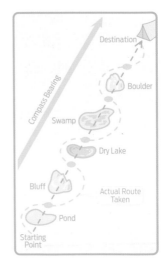

useful when you want to figure out your exact location on the map through triangulation.

SIMPLE TRIANGULATION

There are times when you know roughly where you are but can't pinpoint your location exactly because the land is fairly featureless close by. This may happen in the middle of a glacier or during a crossing of a lake. In this case you can triangulate—or use the intersection of two bearings shot from distant landmarks—to home in on your location.

Start by orienting your map. Then choose two known, visible locations such as a mountain or obvious low pass. Shoot a bearing off this landmark. Keeping the needle boxed, lower your compass onto the map, placing the edge of the base plate through the center of the landmark you just sighted. Draw a line along the edge of the compass through the landmark extending toward you. Your location is on this line somewhere.

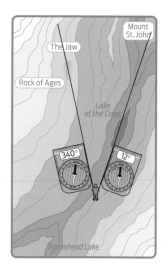

Now pick a second landmark and repeat

the process. The two lines should intersect at your location.

You can also use linear landmarks—say a river or ridge—as one of your triangulation lines. Then you just need to shoot one bearing off a known landmark. The intersection of that bearing and the river or ridge where you are traveling will be your location.

ALTIMETERS

Altimeters measure barometric pressure and translate that information into an elevation reading. As you climb up in elevation, the barometric pressure falls and the altimeter reflects the change, calculating your elevation as you go. If you have a general sense of where you are on the map—say you know you are midway up Mount Baker—an altimeter reading allows you to pinpoint your elevation. Once you locate the contour line for that specific elevation on the map, you know where you are.

Altimeters vary in their reliability and precision. Many people have watches that calculate elevation, as well as pace, distance, even heart rates. These watches work fairly well, but they can be sensitive to weather changes, which also cause the barometric pressure to rise and fall. You may need to recalibrate your altimeter to match your current location, and you may also want to bring along extra batteries to ensure it works when you need it. Mechanical altimeters are more reliable but less durable than electric ones.

In general, altimeters are not necessary for most back-country travelers, so don't feel compelled to go out and buy one unless you are planning to be at high elevations where accuracy is vital. If you happen to own a watch with an altimeter built in, you can play around with it and use it to fine-tune your navigation. If your watch shows a rise in elevation and you haven't even left camp, you can guess a low-pressure system is moving your way and the weather is probably going to deteriorate.

Chapter Four
Dividing the World

Since people began exploring and mapping the world, they have worked to devise systems for codifying locations—grids for dividing the Earth into uniform pieces. The ancient Greek geographer Ptolemy created his own grid system, listing coordinates for places throughout the known world, but it wasn't until the Middle Ages that one system—latitude and longitude—was adopted universally.

In the 1940s the United States Army Corps of Engineers developed another grid system—Universal Transverse Mercator (UTM)—that relied on uniform squares and was based on the number 10, which makes calculations simpler than latitude/longitude, which is based on 60 divisions per unit. UTM has become commonly used today in conjunction with Global Positioning System receivers, or GPS.

LATITUDE AND LONGITUDE

Latitude/longitude was the first universal grid system used for dividing up the Earth and is still used by pilots, sailors, and many GPS users. However, it is more cumbersome than UTM and is therefore becoming less useful for backcountry travelers. Still, it is helpful to understand the basics of lat/long.

Lines of latitude run parallel to the equator. Lines of longitude run north-south and intersect at the poles.

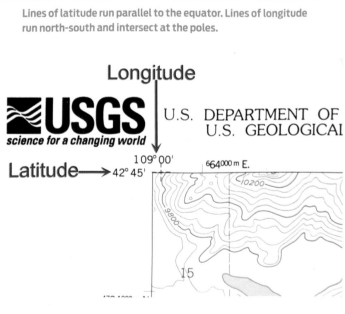

What Are Latitude and Longitude?

Anyone who has spun a globe around has seen the lines of latitude and longitude dividing up the earth.

Latitude lines ascend and descend from the equator in horizontal bands starting with 0° at the equator and ending at 90° at the poles. To help you remember, think of latitude lines as the horizontal rungs of a ladder (ladder-tude). These lines help identify your position north to south.

Longitude lines—also known as meridians—radiate out east and west for 180° from the Prime Meridian, which runs through Greenwich, England. The meridians meet in the middle of the Pacific Ocean at the International Date Line. Longitude is used to locate your position east to west.

Latitude and longitude lines are measured in degrees, minutes, and seconds. One degree equals sixty minutes, one minute equals sixty seconds.

Latitude lines are evenly spaced, and therefore, degrees of latitude represent a constant distance regardless of your location. Longitude is trickier because the north-south lines bend to meet at the poles, and as a result, a degree of longitude represents a varying distance on the ground, depending on your latitude. The further north you are, the more severe the effect on latitude.

Plotting Your Location Using Latitude/Longitude

Measurements of latitude appear in the left and right margins of USGS maps, and measurements of longitude appear on the top and the bottom. Black tick marks along the borders of the map indicate 2.5-minute intervals, and black crosses appear within the map where lat/long lines intersect. To help make it easier to identify your location using lat/long, you can use a straightedge to connect these marks and create a grid on your map.

UNIVERSAL TRANSVERSE MERCATOR (UTM)

What is UTM?

The UTM grid system divides the world into sixty zones that run north/south. These lines are intersected by latitude lines, creating a numbered grid with each square representing one-square kilometer. Because the UTM grid is based on uniform squares and uses base-ten math, it is simpler to use with a GPS than latitude/longitude.

On USGS maps the UTM coordinates are located in the upper left and bottom right corners. They appear like this: $^{6}64^{000m}$E, and $^{47}34^{000m}$N and are expressed as the "easting" and "northing" values. The digits that represent thousand of meters and tens of thousands of meters are enlarged to help you quickly locate which kilometer reference line to use.

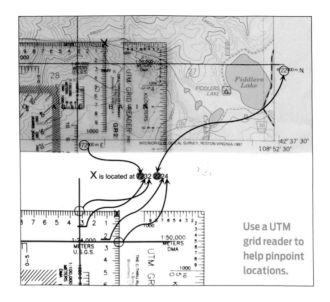

X is located at 72 32 22 24

Use a UTM grid reader to help pinpoint locations.

UTM is rapidly replacing lat/long for travelers seeking precision and ease in their navigation because it provides a constant distance between all points on any USGS map, whereas lat/long varies depending on your latitude.

Reading UTM Coordinates

In order to read and plot UTM coordinates accurately, it helps either to have a UTM grid reader (see illustration) or to have the grid drawn on your map. Some USGS maps come with the UTM grid printed on them, but most do not. Using a straightedge, you can draw the grid yourself by connecting the UTM ticks printed in blue along the borders.

Datum

The datum or dated map data set for your map must be included when using UTM. This information appears in the block of text at the lower left-hand corner of USGS maps and may be the North American Datum 1927, the National Geodetic Vertical Datum of 1929, the North American Datum 1983 or the World Geodetic System 1934. Online mapping tools such as Google Maps commonly use the World Geodetic Systems 1984 (WGS 84) so WGS 84 is becoming the most commonly used reference. Entering the wrong datum for the map you are using is the most common GPS error. For example a WGS 84 coordinate taken from Google Earth or a website and manually entered into a GPS set to NAD 27 datum can be off by close to a mile. Match your datums. Datum mix ups can also cause confusion if you are trying to give information on your location to a pilot or rescue team.

Chapter Five
Global Positioning Systems (GPS)

The Global Positioning System (GPS) uses satellite signals to pinpoint your location wherever you may be. Today's pocket-sized receivers can tell you where you are to within 10 feet in a matter of seconds. Many units on the market today are capable of storing hundreds of locations in their memory, can calculate both the distances you've hiked and your average hiking speed, and can even point you in the direction you want to go. It's a great tool but requires some skill to use and should not be considered a replacement for good map-reading skills.

HOW A GPS WORKS

The U.S. Department of Defense launched the first GPS satellites in 1978. Today GPS technology is not limited to the military, and the system is used for mapping and surveying; to navigate automobiles, ships, airplanes, and boats; and in mining, forestry, agriculture, and many other fields. The first handheld GPS

receivers were introduced in 1989, and backcountry travelers quickly adopted the technology to aid in backcountry navigation.

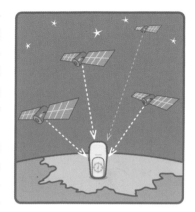

GPS receivers pick up signals from a network of twenty-four satellites circling the earth twice a day. Most units will acquire signals from at least three satellites within three minutes of being turned on. This is known as getting a position fix. For your GPS to work well, it must operate in 3-D mode, which requires signals from a minimum of four satellites. In most places this is not a problem, however, tight canyons and dense forest canopy may cause enough interference to block the signals. If you have less than four signals, your receiver will be functioning in 2-D mode, which is less accurate. In fact, readings may be off by as much as a mile in 2-D, so it is important for you to know what mode you are in before you begin plotting your position.

The receiver measures the signals it receives and basically triangulates the messages to calculate your position. Each position fix is displayed in either UTM coordinates or in latitude/longitude.

ENTERING WAYPOINTS

Waypoints are representations of points on the earth that are stored in your GPS's memory. By guiding you from waypoint to waypoint, your receiver can aid in route finding. Entering waypoints creates a route description or record of the places you've visited. Waypoints can be stored in two ways: By entering the coordinates manually or by pushing a sequence of buttons to record a snapshot of your physical location in the receiver's memory.

This information is valuable for a variety of purposes. A friend may give you waypoints for a rendezvous spot, a hidden campsite, or perhaps a secret fishing hole. You can give waypoints to a pilot coming

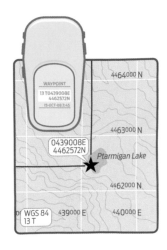

in to pick you up or take out an injured hiker. You can also enter the way-points into your GPS and then push the "Go To" function. This brings up an arrow that directs you to that point.

Remember that the GPS does not recognize hazardous terrain, so the Go To arrow may take you right to the edge of a cliff or an impassable canyon. If you are forced to turn off the direct linear route by such an obstacle, the GPS will adjust and correct your line.

If you make a habit of recording waypoints while traveling, your GPS will enable you to retrace your route—linking the points you passed before—even if you are in complete darkness or a blinding blizzard. Entering your waypoints does not require plotting or entering numbers but merely pressing a sequence of buttons under the waypoint menu in your receiver.

SO WHY PLOT COORDINATES?

If the GPS can do it all, why bother learning how to plot coordinates? The answer is so you can interface with your map.

You need to know how to plot either UTM or latitude/longitude coordinates on your map to interpret the readings you are receiving from your GPS and find your location in the physical world around you. Furthermore, GPS receivers aren't good route finders: they won't tell you the best way to get from point A to point B, and they can't identify a nice place to camp or a good peak to climb.

To travel effectively in the backcountry, you should rely on your map first and foremost, and use your GPS to enhance your precision and communicate your location to others.

COMMON ERRORS OR PROBLEMS

A GPS receiver's accuracy can be affected by either "multipath interference" or "selective unavailability."

Multipath interference happens when a signal bounces off an object such as a cliff or a building on its way to your receiver. It's hard to tell if this has affected your reading, so to be on the safe side, stay away from cliffs when taking a position fix in the backcountry.

Selective unavailability is intentional GPS error introduced by the U.S. military operators of the GPS satellite system to limit the level of accuracy available to military adversaries. The primary effect of SU is to distort position fixes, speed over ground, and direction of travel in selected areas of the globe. It's good to be aware of SU, but for civilian backcountry users, it is not a problem unless you are traveling through war zones or in politically sensitive areas.

Probably your biggest potential problem is going to be battery power. Low battery power can cause GPSs to malfunction, so bring lots of spares if you plan to use your receiver frequently. Make sure you know whether your receiver is waterproof. If it is not, carry the unit in a plastic bag to keep moisture out. Finally, protect your transceiver from extreme temperatures, both hot and cold. Again, such conditions may affect the GPS's ability to function, and it may give you inaccurate readings or perhaps fail to work at all.

Chapter Six
Route Finding

Most backcountry travelers get into trouble when they get lost, overestimate their abilities, encounter unexpected hazards or weather, or get injured. There's not a lot that good backcountry navigation skills can do to avoid some of these situations. Reading a map may not help you anticipate a blizzard or keep you from spraining your ankle, but it does allow you to recognize where you are, calculate the difficulty of your objective, and anticipate many potential hazards.

PLANNING AHEAD

One of the best exercises I've seen for helping beginning backcountry travelers hone their navigation skills is having them write a daily travel plan. This may sound ridiculous, but generating a written plan for your day forces you to look at your map closely, examine the route carefully, and consider everything from handrails and landings to potential hazards and estimated travel times. Therefore, I highly recommend that new backcountry travelers write daily travel plans, and experienced ones take the time to go through their route verbally before starting out each day.

A travel plan contains the following information:

Travel Plan

» Starting point and estimated time of departure
» Description of destination
» Distance (include linear distance plus elevation gain)
» Estimated travel time
» Detailed route description (include handrails and landings and estimated arrival times at these points)
» Potential hazards (river crossings, boulder fields, snow, and so on)
» Estimated arrival time

<u>Start Time</u>: 8:00 AM

Estimate hiking Speed: 2 miles per hour

Linear Mileage : 11 miles

Elevation   : 1500 foot gain

Break Times : 15 minutes/hour

Potential Campsite : Meadow on north end of Tom's Lake

Attraction/Hazards: Boulderfield near Bear Mountain

<u>Ending Time</u> : 5:00 PM

<u>Route description</u>

- Start at Big Opening trail head
- Hike north along trail for 3 miles
    - Cross Fish Creek
- At the junction of Popo Agie River stay on the north side of River and follow unmarked trail to East for 4,
- At the base of Bear Mountain go through boulder field to the south for approximately ½ mile and join Middle Fork Trail
- Travel north for 4.5 miles miles - passed Tom's Lake to meadow on north end of lake — CAMP

Travel plans are both a great way to familiarize yourself with your route and a way to let others know where to look in case of an emergency.

ON-TRAIL TRAVEL

Trails are planned and built by professionals, so while they do not always follow the shortest path from point A to point B, they tend to be situated along the safest, most environmentally sensitive line, so do your best to stay on the trail. Sticking to the main trail is also the best way to minimize your impact on the natural world. You've probably crossed meadows laced with parallel tracks where hikers or horsepackers have traveled abreast or spread out to go around mud. To avoid the proliferation of such trails, travel single file in the main track of the trail. Wear gaiters so you can walk through puddles without getting your feet wet, and avoid shortcuts.

Following a trail, even a well-maintained trail, is not always as easy as you expect, however. Sometimes side trails form from hiker traffic leading off to unknown points—a fishing hole or climbing route, for example—making it difficult to recognize the main path. Other times mud, snow, or fallen trees block the main trail, and you head off into the brush, only to find you cannot relocate the trail on the other side. Or you may find yourself above treeline moving over boulders where it is difficult to tell exactly where to go.

If you come to an obstacle such as a snowbank or fallen tree and cannot see where the trail continues on the other side, have one person in your party stay on the known trail while others scout to reloc...

the trail further along. This trick helps whenever you find yourself unsure of where to go.

In some places trails traverse bare rock or boulders; in these situations you will usually be able to locate some kind of physical trail marker such as a stack of rocks known as a cairn or a mark painted on the rock to indicate the path. In many forested areas, slashes on trees or blazes are used to mark the path. If in doubt, look at your map. Usually, you can tell where the logical line of travel will be and will be able to locate the trail again if you've lost it because of obstacles or indistinct markings.

Try to travel at a comfortable pace—one at which you can carry on a conversation, look at the scenery, and identify landmarks without getting out of breath. You'll find you are able to travel for longer distances without a break if you maintain a steady, rhythmic pace. If you've ever followed someone who

Cairns, or piles of rock, are often used to mark trails in open areas.

is constantly stopping to adjust a strap, talk about his job or love life, sip some water, or turn to ask you a question, you know how hard it is to hike all day in a stop-and-go manner.

Experiment with different walking techniques. On flat trail your best bet is to walk flat-footed in loosely laced boots. This prevents excessive motion in your shoes, thereby helping to prevent blisters from

Good hiking techniques—such as sidestepping up steep slopes—can help improve your stability and balance and make traveling with a pack easier on your knees.

Take rest breaks off the trail so you don't get in the way of other hikers. Use the time to check your map and make sure you know where you are.

forming. Shorter steps can reduce stress on your joints and muscles, especially when you are traveling downhill. Use your eyes. Just like skiers and boaters pick their lines before descending a mogul field or rapid, hikers should consciously pick each foot placement to avoid awkward movements and precarious positions. Ski poles are helpful for maintaining balance and to lessen the strain on your knees. And sidestepping on steep terrain improves balance and footing.

Try to take rest breaks away from and, if possible, out of sight of the trail. This helps preserve the sense of solitude both for yourself and for others who might pass while you are eating lunch or taping a blister.

Rest Step

On steep slopes the "rest step" allows you to conserve energy and travel efficiently. To use the rest step, take a step uphill. Straighten your downhill leg at the knee, and shift all your weight onto it, pausing to rest momentarily. Now step up onto the uphill leg, swing your other leg past so it becomes the uphill one, and shift all your weight onto the new downhill leg. Straighten this leg at the knee and pause to rest before repeating. When done correctly, the rest step allows you to travel at a steady, rhythmic pace for long periods of time up steep inclines without undue exertion.

OFF-TRAIL TRAVEL

In some parts of the world, cross-country travel is impossible or unpleasant because of thick vegetation or boggy soil. But in other places off-trail travel is more reasonable and enjoyable for experienced navigators. Don't leave the trails behind if you do not have excellent map-reading skills, however; that's just asking for trouble.

Start planning your off-trail day the same way you plan for a day of trail hiking: Look at your map and come up with a detailed travel plan. The big difference is that you, not the trail builders, will be picking your route, so you need to become familiar with what makes a good line of travel. I usually look for ridges to follow or gradual slopes to contour around. Drainages make great handrails, but watch out for tight valleys—you may find yourself scrambling along steep banks or wading in the river trying to stay along the streambed.

Watch for potential obstacles, and look to make sure there are no "stoppers" along your line. Do you come to a cliff where the contour lines disappear? There's no way you'll be able to get around that kind of obstacle without a rope, so make sure you have options. Does your path descend into a deep canyon? Again, without a boat, you may find yourself unable to proceed on this line.

Often you know you've picked a good path when you find yourself following wild animal trails. Stick with them; they usually know the best line for moving through the mountains.

NEGOTIATING POTENTIAL OBSTACLES

Rocky Terrain

When you travel in the mountains, you are almost guaranteed to encounter some rocky terrain: boulder fields, scree slopes, or unstable moraines are commonly found in alpine areas.

Boulder fields can be fun once you gain some confidence moving across them.

Look ahead and pick out the easiest line of travel when crossing boulders. Use your hands for stability.

Stop and assess your "line" across the boulders. Look for flat, smaller boulders, and try to seek the most level terrain. Walk slowly but smoothly, and avoid jumping. Don't walk with anything in your hands so you are free to use them for balance. Ski poles can be tricky in boulder fields. I generally put mine away for this kind of travel. Beware, rocks can move when you step on them, so try to avoid placing all your weight along one edge or in between boulders where your foot can get pinned.

Scree or talus slopes (scree usually refers to smaller-sized rocks, but some people use the terms interchangeably) are loose piles of rock that shift and slide when you walk through them. Your best bet in scree is to ascend in a parallel line, so no member of

Warning

Beware, scrambling up rocky terrain is easier than moving down through it. So don't strand yourself halfway up a cliff unable to descend. The minute you start using your hands to move, stop and ask yourself, am I willing and able to reverse this move? Is there another way down?

Sometimes you will find you are uncomfortable facing out as you descend over exposed terrain. You'll feel safer and more balanced if you turn in and down climb. You may also opt to do a "butt slide" in places, but be careful: Reversing a butt slide is not always possible, especially if it involves a little jump to reach the ground below. Still, sliding off a rock on your rear end is a lot more controllable and safer than jumping down.

your team is below in your rock fall zone. Kick steps in the scree, and switchback your way up the slope, gathering your group at each end of your switchback to avoid traveling above others.

To descend scree, head straight down the slope, kicking your heels in a plunge step. Again, travel side by side with your companions, and beware of people below. Rock fall hazard is very real in this terrain. If you do kick off a rock, scream "Rock!" until you hear or see an acknowledgment that anyone in potential danger has heard you and moved out of the way.

Snow

If you hike in the Rocky Mountains or the Sierras, you are likely to cross snow regardless of the season. Winter snows begin accumulating in October and often don't melt out until well into June, and permanent snowfields are found in the high peaks year-round. Traveling across snow can be fun and easy; it can also be deceptively dangerous, but there are some techniques that can help minimize the hazard.

Winter and early spring snow is often soft, so you may find yourself flailing your way through thigh-deep snow if you do not have on snowshoes or skis. Most spring backcountry travelers opt to bring snowshoes along to avoid postholing. As the season progresses you may decide it isn't worth the weight of snowshoes for the few patches of soft snow you will encounter. In this situation you may find it easier to

Use kick steps in a gradual line up a snow slope for easy travel. Make sure you have a good runout—or can stop yourself—if you do slip and fall.

travel in the early morning before the sun softens the snow. Look for shady spots where the snow may stay harder longer, or walk along the edges of snow patches where it isn't as deep.

Summer snow is usually hard and old, so your best method for traveling is to use a kick step to ascend and the plunge step to descend.

You'll find stiff boots work best for kicking effective steps. The basic technique is to angle your way up the slope, kicking your uphill boot into the snow to create a stable platform at least half the width of your foot. Try swinging from your knee to get some momentum behind your kick. If the slope gets steeper and the snow is soft, you can face in and kick straight in, ascending the snow like a ladder.

Keep "your nose over your toes," and kick your feet aggressively into the snow when descending.

To descend, face out and kick your heels into the snow deeply. Remember to lean forward enough to keep "your nose over your toes." If you lean back, your feet are likely to shoot out from under you, leaving you sliding downhill on your bottom, which is another way to descend! You can glissade on your feet—or boot ski—or slide on your butt down a snow slope, but beware—it is very easy to lose control. You need to know how to stop, and you need to have a safe runout below in case your self-arrest techniques fail.

Beware of icy patches or places where you cannot get good purchase for your feet. It is all too easy to find yourself suddenly stranded in the middle of a snowfield that has turned out to be steeper and icier than you anticipated. Always assess your runout before you begin crossing snow. Make sure that if you fall and are unable to stop you are not going to end

To self-arrest with an ice ax, grasp the ax across your chest with one hand on the head, the other on the shaft. Roll onto your stomach, and dig the pick of the ax into the snow, while simultaneously kicking your toes in until you come to a stop.

Stopping on Snow

If you anticipate crossing a lot of snow, it's worth taking some time to practice basic self-arrest techniques and to consider carrying an ice ax.

The most effective technique *without* an ice ax is to roll onto your stomach, dig your hands into the snow, and kick your feet in.

If you have an ice ax, hold it with two hands across your chest and dig into the snow with your pick, kicking in your feet at the same time to slow yourself down.

These techniques work best in soft snow. They become less reliable when the snow is hard or you are sliding very quickly. Make sure to stop yourself before there is a lot of momentum behind your fall, and avoid hard, icy snow if you do not have the appropriate equipment.

up sliding into boulders or over a cliff. If the runout is not safe, do not ascend or descend the slope.

River Crossings

River crossings are one of the most dangerous things you will do in the backcountry. Swift cold water, slippery rocks, strainers, and rapids can all make a fall uncomfortable at best, deadly at worst.

Obviously, the risk involved in crossing a river is situational. Late summer travel often means nothing more than some rock hopping over sluggish creeks, but early spring frequently means high water levels and frigid temperatures. Under these conditions, river crossings must be taken seriously.

Scout river crossings thoroughly before committing yourself. Ideally, you are looking for a place where the river spreads out, the current is less pushy, and there are no downstream hazards, such as strainers or rapids. Check your map. Meadows often make

Potential River Hazards

» **Strainers:** Downed trees across rivers create deadly traps for swimmers. Water moves under and through these obstacles and can pin a person against the branches. Avoid strainers at all costs! If you cannot, swim directly at the obstacle, and try to use your momentum to climb up on top of the downed tree.

» **Swift Water:** Rapidly moving water above knee height is enough to knock most people over. Do not underestimate the power of water. Before you commit yourself to a crossing, determine water depth and speed.

» **Floating Logs:** Watch out for obstacles floating downstream, especially in the early season during runoff.

» **Rocks:** Rocks can be slippery and treacherous. Make sure you cross in boots or sturdy shoes to help stabilize your foot placements. Foot entrapment—where your foot is stuck between rocks—can be very dangerous, as the force of the water can make it difficult to dislodge your foot and keep your head above water if you should fall.

» **Cold Water:** Cold water numbs your feet, saps your strength, and can lead to hypothermia if you aren't careful. Don't cross in bare feet. If it's chilly, wear your polypropylene bottoms to maintain some warmth. Take time to warm up after you cross, especially on cold, wet days.

good crossing spots because the water slows down as it travels over more level terrain. The river may be deep, but the force of the current will be gentle, making it easier to cross.

You can also travel upstream, above river junctions, so you can cross smaller tributaries rather than trying to ford the main current. The more tributaries you cross, the less volume you will encounter in any given channel. This is also the case in braided rivers, and you have the added advantage of resting on gravel bars midstream.

In addition to scouting the water conditions, make sure you check for easy paths in and out of the river. It does you no good to have the perfect crossing if it leads to a steep, muddy bank with no way out.

Crossing Techniques

» **Dry Crossings:** No one likes to get his or her feet wet, so most of us look for some kind of bridge to get us across without dampening our feet. Unfortunately, the bigger the river, the harder it is to find a safe, dry crossing. Logs, whether singular or several jammed together, are often ideal, but make sure you'll be okay if you slip and fall, and remember that wet trees are slippery. You may want to set up a handline between trees to give people some stability as they traverse.

» **Wet Crossings:** Often the only way to get across a river is to wade.

Factors to Keep in Mind Before Wading

» Water depth
» Speed of the current
» Water temperature
» Distance across
» What's on the river bottom
» What's downstream

Before you plunge into the river blindly, you should prepare. Take off your rain or wind pants—anything that can catch the current and cause resistance. Make sure you don't have gaiter straps hanging off or loose shoelaces that can trip you up. Consider unbuckling your hip belt. Some people believe this helps you escape an unwieldy pack if you do fall and have to swim to safety. Others advocate keeping your pack on for flotation. If you anticipate lots of deep-water crossings on your expedition, it's worth practicing both with and without your pack to see what feels most comfortable. Any crossing that is knee deep or greater has the potential to be dangerous, so do not underestimate the hazard, and plan accordingly.

Crossing Strategies

» Face upstream. Use a hefty stick to create a third point of contact and help maintain

You can use people to act as a kind of human eddy for crossing turbulent water.

balance. Move one foot, then the other, then the stick—one thing at a time.

» Don't stare at the current; it can be mesmerizing and may cause you to lose your balance.

» Sidestep across, shuffling rather than crossing your feet, again to maximize your balance.

» Help each other out. Hold hands or link arms for stability while crossing, or reach back to help your teammates through tricky spots.

» Cross in a group, placing your largest team member in front of a line to form a kind of human eddy. Smaller people can stand behind, holding tightly to the person in front and walking sideways in unison across the river.

» If there is really a good chance that someone in your group could end up swimming, it's smart to position a spotter downstream to help your colleague to shore.

» Wear boots or tennis shoes unless the river is sandy bottomed and very gentle. Otherwise, you'll want the protection and support of shoes when stepping on and around slippery rocks.

Weather

There is a reason mountain climbers like to get a pre-dawn start on their day: afternoon thunderstorms. If you've ever experienced the buzzing of a nearby

The key to the lightning position is to minimize your contact with the ground to avoid ground current. Try to make yourself small so you are lower than the objects around you.

electric storm, you know it's not a great feeling, especially when you are exposed on a mountaintop.

Plan your day to avoid high passes or summits in the afternoon. Watch for afternoon buildup or the gradual accumulation of clouds as the day progresses. Try to head down if you see a storm coming.

If you do get trapped in a lightning storm, what should you do? First, figure out how serious the situation is. Count the number of seconds between the lightning flash and the boom of thunder. Five seconds roughly equates to one mile. Obviously, if you are not getting to five in your count, you'd better take some precautions immediately. Your best bet is to find some place of equal coverage, ideally, a thick forest where no one tree stands out as a lightning rod. If this is impossible, try to avoid being the highest point. Spread your group out, and assume the lightning position: sit curled up tightly on your pack or a sleeping pad—keep your feet tucked up next to your body **minimizing your exposure to ground current**.

If you do not have a pack, pad, or something else to sit on, squat down holding your knees to your chest. Again, try to minimize your exposure to ground current, and wait for the storm to pass.

INDEX

altimeter, 4, 7, 42–43
  mechanical, 42

barometric pressure, 42
bearing, shoot a, 7,
  39–40
bezel, 34, 39
boulder fields, 63–64
boxing the needle, 34–
  35, 39

cairn, 59
compass, 4, 5, 34–42
  bezel, 34, 39
  boxing the needle,
    34–35, 39
  direction of travel
    arrow, 34, 35–36,
    39, 40
  magnetic needle, 5
  magnetic north, 5
contour line(s), 8, 11,
  17–18, 20, 21, 42
coordinates, why plot,
  53–54

datum, 49
  See also National
    Geodetic Vertical
    Datum of 1929, 49
  North American
    Datum 1927, 49
  North American
    Datum 1983, 49
  World Geodetic
    System 1984 (WGS
    84), 49
declination, 35–36
  diagram, 14
degrees, 46
direction, sense of, 3
direction of travel arrow,
  34, 35–36, 39, 40

elevation, 42
elevation point, 7
equator, 46

Global Positioning
  System (GPS), 4, 5,
  44, 49, 50–55
  2–D mode, 51
  3–D mode, 51

battery, low, 55
entering waypoints, 52–53
Go To arrow, 53
how it works, 50–51
position fix, 51
problems with, 54–55
Google Earth, 49
Google maps, 49
Greenwich, England, 46
grid(s), 44, 47
Grid North, 15

index contour, 17
International Date Line, 46

knuckle mountain, how to make, 18–19

landforms, 8,
recognizing, 19–22
latitude, 44–47, 51
lightning, what to do, 77–78
location, determining, 22
longitude, 44–47, 51

magnetic north, 15, 36
map
bearing from, 39–41
datum, 49
orientation, 37, 41
meridians, 46
minutes, 46
multipath interference, 54

National Geodetic Vertical Datum of 1929, 49
National Map program, *see* United States Geological Survey (USGS) maps
natural world, minimizing impact on, 58
navigation
clues, 3
direction, sense of, 3
key signs of, 3
plan ahead, 56–57
sun in, 3
travel plan, 56–57
navigation tools
altimeter, 4

compass, 4, 5
GPS, 4, 7
intuition, 4
topographic map, 5
North American Datum
   1927, 49
North American Datum
   1983, 49
North Star, 3

obstacles, travel
   river crossings, 70–76
   rocky terrain, 63–66
   snow, 66–70
   weather, 76–78
off–trail travel, 62–63
on–trail travel, 58–61

Prime Meridian, 46
Ptolemy, 44

river crossings, 70–76
   hazards, 71
   strategies, 74–76
   techniques, 72–74
route
   anticipating hazards,
      27–29

calculating travel
   time, 25–26
measuring distance,
   25
planning, 22–29

satellite signals, 50–51
scale, 11
scree, 64–65
seconds, 46
selective unavailability,
   54
snow, self arrest
   techniques, 69
   with ice ax, 69
summer snow, 67

talus, see scree
topographic map, 8–33
   care of maps, 31–33
   common map–
      reading mistakes,
      29–30
   folding, 32–33
   other types of
      maps, 31

planning a route,
22–29
reading, 11–16
using, 17–22
topographic map,
information about
color, 15
common symbols, 16
declination
diagram, 14
importance of date
of, 11
scale, 11
travel time, calculating,
25–26
triangulation, 41–42, 51
true north, 14, 35–36,
37, 39

United States Army
Corps of Engineers,
44
United States Geological
Survey (USGS) maps,
9, 47
1:24,000–scale, 9
7.5 minute, 9, 17
National Map
program, 9

Universal Transverse
Mercator (UTM), 44,
47–49
map coordinates,
47–49, 51
UTM grid reader, 48
U.S. Department of
Defense, 50
U.S. military, 50, 54–55

walking techniques,
60–61, 62
butt slide, 65
flat–footed, 60
kick step, 67
plunge step, 67
rest step, 62
short steps, 61
sidestepping, 61
waypoints, entering,
52–53
weather, 76–78
lightning, 77–78
World Geodetic System
1984 (WGS 84), 49